WEATHER-BEAM

Previous Publications

WEATHER-BEAM

Tricia Jones

ACKNOWLEDGEMENTS

Guardian Angel
Like a beam from above
In these troubled times
A white dove.

CONTENTS

Blow

You are gone
In a whisper
Of the night
You make yourself
Aware of your
Presence, flaunting
Yourself, safe
Comforting, a little
Suspicious then fate
Takes a hand, one minute
You are there, the next the
Shadow has gone, I look
Around and can't understand
Where you could have gone
A flicker of a candle
Then the gentle hum of
Voices go in a puff of
Smoke, army training.

Weather-Beam

Roaring towards you
Diminishing into bubbles
The water drawing back
As more waves follow
The beach is covered
Looking like snow
Until the blue water
Is left behind
A rope attached to the lower corner of a sail
The part of a boat between the thwarts and the stern or bow
The sky is crimson
A fire-breathing dragon, a luminous phenomenon,
A primitive instrument for making fire by twirling a stick
Glowing appearance, a sparkle of light
Refraction of light in a gem stone.

1

Toast

After warm sunny days
Jack Frost
Bites his lip
And everything in the garden
Is sprayed
By the ice-maiden
The birds eagerly
In the trees
Wait to be fed
While we are having
Hot toast inside.

Cold-Cloud

The rain is like ice
With wet gloves
Smearing your nose
Pulling woollen hat over freezing ears
Shiver down your spine
Wipes nose
The sun
Like a fire-ball
All of a sudden
Rainbow chaser
Someone who tries to reach the end of the rainbow
To pursue an impossible aim
A form of colour therapy
Based on drinking water
That is considered to have taken on
The energy specific to the colour of its container
Of, or coloured like, the rainbow
Attempting to cause rainfall by techniques such as seeding clouds
A little pit made by a raindrop in clay
Keeps moving
Where is that pot of gold
And why?

Forever

God is always with us
We are not alone
In this never ending universe.

Taste

I sniff lovely smells
Coming from
The oven
It is Sunday
And my husband is cooking
And the main meal
I can taste in
The air
Just before
It is served.

New Start

Clean shirt and collar
In the hope
Of leading
A better life
Enthusiasm
Vitality
Energy
Mixing with others
Refreshed
With the knowledge
That somebody cares.

Missing Link

With the
Swaying
Of the world
When will it
Give people
A better chance
And the possibility
Of mixing with others
Instead of being frightened
And looking over your shoulder.

Tag

When you
Care for others
It is not enough
Because
The bullies
Always win.

World

Companionship
Is the greatest
Thing in the world
And yet
Other people
Are tearing it apart.

The Wait

The ticking
Of the clock
In time and space
When you are
In thought
Time drags
How can we make it
A better world.

Survival

The trees
In winter
Bend to the wind
Icicles appear
As spider webs
And dew drops
Protect themselves
From the storms
Squirrels eating nuts
Down the garden path
In time for tea.

Friend

In our darkest moments
Christ is our only hope
Although he may seem
A million miles away
He is with us
His Angels are all around us
We are not alone
He is watching
And although it may seem
We are on our own
We must cling to the thought
People are worse off than us
And always manage a smile
It may be a tough world
But think of the afterlife
The mysterious and unknown
All that He has created
We love you Lord.

Forever

God is with you
Wherever you go
He sends His Angels
To surround you and protect you.

Freedom

Powdered silk
The sand like
Soft flour
Beautiful, gushing
Roaring, slintering into foam
Of the waves
A deep green, overturning
On the cold flat beach
Or letting their birds-nest hair
Blow freely in the wind
Sandy wet feet
Cleansed by the tide.

Him

Your love
Is like a
Red, red rose
Squeeze the petals
And you get an aroma
Of sweet perfume
Scented in the spray
Of a thousand
Bluebells
Ringing their bells
In the morning sun.

Audience

The sea roars
And talks
To the mer-folks
Anger from the pebbles
As they applaud
The fresh green waves.

Indoors

Snowflakes fall
Like an army
Of busy bees
In a wild frenzy
The roofs are slowly turning white
Cars are busy down the main road
Driving conditions are becoming critical
Swimming past the window
White lattice spider webs
People are worrying about getting home
The ice war has begun.

Sunshine

Raw red cheeks
Building snowmen
Trays, boxes and sledges
Carrying eager children
Down a slope
Cries of happiness
In the snow.

Sunday

My happiest moments
Am when I am sitting
Next to you on the settee
You reading your paper
And we both listening to the radio
The back door is open
Where I have put
Bread out for the birds
On the wooden bird table
Sipping tea and
Relaxing.

Forever

With your hand in mine
I could sleep through
A thousand yesterdays.

Together

The wind may blow
Ice through the air
Snug inside
With nothing to fear.

Shadows

As God laughed
The almighty waves
Became into shimmering light.

First

We watched
As the squirrel
Was eating the nuts
A wood pigeon
Flew and sat on the fence nearby
Some action has to be taken
A very tricky situation
The squirrel stamped one of its paws
And the wood pigeon flew away.

Cobweb

Why does God
Hurt
But it is
Manmade
And we must
Help one another
To get through
Troubles
Tears
Help melt a
Heart of stone
We must never
Stop believing
In His almighty power but
Also His sensitivity of a Father
Through the snow-storm we survive.

Raw

A tear drop
Fell down
The face
And turned
Into an icicle
To hide his sorrow.

Chatter

Little Robin
Perched on the
Garden wall. In his
Mouth is a large piece
Of bread that I've
Put out on the bird
Table. His friend the
House-martin had some
Bread in his beak
Too. Thank you
Little birds fly
Away
Safe.

Fire-Light

Your love and support
Is all I need
In a hug,
Safe, warm
Relaxing
The fire-light glows
And the television
Stills the silence
With its soaps
With the world outside
In the dark
We are sitting snug
In each other's arms
Toes feeling the heat
Of the coal fire.

Wonderland

Running along the sands
Wet feet
Shapes in the sand
White foam
Crashing on the shore
People are dancing
In my mind
But only bird prints
Can be seen along the sands
The rocks glisten
In happiness
As they are washed
By the tide.

Sunset

Fingers touch the water
And blisters are healed
Seagulls flying high
Above the blue water
The sand is covered by crystal seas
Sparkled by the
Evening
Sun.

Music

The foam surrounds you
And cleanses your feet
Icy chill, goose-bubbles
Silver crashing on the shore.

The Tide

Like a mirror
Different colours roll over
The sand is yellow
And shadows fade away
As the tide draws back
Pink, green and blue shells
Are left behind.

Diamond

You are my
Soul-mate
The
One
I am
Wedded
To.
Without
You this
World
Would be
A grim place
My
Children
And Grandson
And family
Are my
Life and I
Owe it all
To the
Lord.

Imperfect

An odd specie
Is terminated
By the perfect.

Harp-Seal

The sunset
Purple twinkling
Sparkling from the sea
The music of the waves
Are like birds singing
A grey animal with
Dark bands curved like
An old harp
A musical instrument played by
Plucking strings stretched from
A curved neck to an inclined
Sound-board
A harmonica, mouth-organ
To the washing on the shore
Covering the beach
Birds ride on waves of pure silk
The melody will wash
Away our fears
The rocks are sound
As they stand solid
Until night falls
And they too turn into crimson.

Peace

Heat on hot hands
The crackling of sticks
A furnace
In the sands
The flames
Are like red shadows
Dancing at midnight.

Move

Just half asleep
Hearing the crackling of the coal fire
Sitting together on the fire-side settee
Relaxing
With eyes closed
I hear you turning the pages of your newspaper
Looking especially at the
Sports page
With the hum of television
In the background
Just after a meal of hot apples and custard
Content, comfortable
Finishing the remains
Of a boiling hot cup of tea
Pull hair away from face
And sink into slumber land.

Paddle-Wheel

Pink, whispering
Glistening upon rocks
Soothing, rolling over
Blue sea
A seagull flies past
Flapping its wings
Soaring to depths unknown
A small long-handled spade
A short, broad, spoon-shaped oar,
Used for moving canoes
A swimming animal's flipper
Shore like biscuit
Waiting to be danced upon
To move rhythmically to music
To spring, to cause to dance or jump
What secrets do these waves hold
Bubbles of the surface of a liquid
Birds riding on a line or streak like a wave
A movement of the raised hand expressing greeting
Foam creeping
Washed by the magic of nature
Pulled back by the tide
Wet rocks sparkling
The beach is damp and smooth
Navy blue, waiting to be trodden upon
Paddling in bare feet
Spot-light on the water
The sun twinkles like stars.

Butter-Dish

Flowers grow
When they are watered
And of course
Spoken to, able to speak and write
A particular language
Competently and with ease
Of a movement
Smooth, easy or graceful
A slime fungus
On tan-bark, pool in a swamp
Moist track of land
Wild flowers
To blossom, to flourish
Growing in the long grass
A blossom shared like a bell
A bud with an un-opened flower
Relating to the Goddess Flora,
To floras, or to flowers
Colourfully dressed adherents
Of a cult
The flowery land
I enjoy
Watering them
They seem to
Stretch out
Their petals
And say thank you.

Taste

Melissa was on the phone
It was Easter
And she said that they
Had laid a treasure trail of tiny Easter eggs
For Finn to follow
He is only two and found the first half inch egg
Behind a cushion
And then he found the second chocolate egg
Behind another cushion
He then fond the third in his toy car.
Melissa suddenly said, 'Oh no,' she
Said, 'he is
Looking for more.'

Tapping Feet

Sitting
With Dennis
In the light of the evening
Sun
Music playing, just each other's
Company
Sitting on
A settee made
For two. Cosy
Cushions
There are
Shadows
With your head
On me you are fast
Asleep, relaxing soaking up
Vitamin D.

Hunger-Bitten

The trees are twinkling
In the sun
A lot of dead wood
But it is home to the squirrels
I remember when our cats
Used to sit on one of its branches
And would look down
Enjoying themselves.
The squirrels
Nimble, bushy-tailed
To look obliquely
To have the eyes
Focusing in different directions
Craving for food, need
Or lack of food
Greedy, desirous, longing
Stingy, mean
And hundreds of
Different species of birds
Who compete
To whose turn it is
To eat from the bird table.
Relating to or using sound waves
Any characteristic sound
Suffering from thirst
Dry, parched,
Bird call, a bird's song
A stone mosaic basin set up
For birds to bathe in.

Slipperiness

Why is this
A cold hard world
Where a little
Thought
Could go on
A long way
Bullying has not gone out
With the ark
The vulnerable
Are still around
What is the answer
In these days
Trust in the Lord
But sometimes it is
The hardest
Thing to do.

Him

Cosy
Like a
Hug in a rug
I am so happy
Just being with you
Gives me vibes
Of happiness
Like the warmth
Of the sun
From nature's crust.

Summer

When I wash my hair
I go into the garden
And sit facing the sun
And it blows slightly
And dries my hair
I stare into the face
Of the sun
With my eyes closed.

Restore

I had severe back-ache
So every day I would sit
In the middle of the sun's
Rays showing
A picture of the window
In the centre of my feet
On the floor
Sitting on the windowsill for one minute
Wearing my ordinary clothes
I could feel the sun on my neck
And it moved slowly down my back
And then I relaxed and let the sun do its work
After one minute I would get up
Off the windowsill
I did this every morning for one week
The pain had gone.

Drift'age

A heap of matter
Driven together
Floating materials
Driven by water
A slow current
Caused by the wind
A moveable seat
For one person
With a back, four legs
And sometimes arms
The seat or office of
Someone in authority
Judge, a bishop
Presiding over any meeting
And to sway to and fro
Tilt from side to side
A rocking movement
A person who rocks
An apparatus that rocks
A curved support on which anything rocks
Picking up driftwood
Along the beach
To make a chair
Careful consideration
On what the tide
Has brought in
I sat many a happy hour
Rocking to sleep
Watched by the stars overhead.

Snow-Broth

A dome-shaped but made of blocks of
Hard snow, now a dwelling made of other materials
Fondness, charity
An affection for
Something that gives
Pleasure
A mass or expanse
Of snow
Anything white, such as hair
Atmospheric vapour
Frozen in crystalline form
Whether in single crystals
Or aggregated in flakes
A person who lives
Retired from the world
Seclusion from society
A hole dug in snow
As a temporary shelter
A ball made of snow
Pressed hard together
Used as a missile
A lustre in the
Eye expressing
Love
Staff in hand
In a snowstorm
A boot or overshoe for walking in snow
To draw air in violently
And noisily through the nose
To sniff, to smell at anything doubtfully
Lurking in the shadows
Is a face unseen
But the sun
Keeps smiling on
A feathery clump of
Snow crystals.

Morning-Gift

The sun, the moon
And the stars
To meditate,
To reflect,
Asleep in paradise
Until the early morning sounds
The call of the cuckoo.
Ease of mind
Or conscience
Tranquillity, quiet
Stillness, silence
A dove, a pigeon
A wood-pigeon
A roof gutter or
Groove
A twist of hair at
The
Back
Of the
Head,
Hooded, shaped like a hood,
And the freshness of the garden
Outside.

Seconds

Raining at
Dead of night
Fresh air
Overwhelming rain
The sound of a downpour
The clock keeps ticking
As time stands still
On the hour
It chimes
And every half hour
The minutes
Are drifting by
A cool breeze
Comes through the window
As the damp rain
Refreshes
Your
Soul.

Pets

Our birds let us
Know how much bread
They want us to leave
Them on the bird table
One day I put half a
Loaf broken up on the
Bird table. One hour later
We looked out of our
Window and they had pushed
A lot of the bread onto the
Grass and had ate a little
Bit. So the next week
I just put three slices of
Broken bread on the bird table
In the trees,
To look narrowly or closely
To look with strain
Or with half-closed eyes
To peep, to appear,
One hour later we went out
And the birds had eaten it.
Communication. We also put
Out seeds on the table
And some on the grass that is
Eagerly eaten. They sing
So beautifully and we see
Many different species of
Birds plus the squirrels.

Windowless

A pane of glass
In a window
A seat below a window
In a bay or alcove
Look at goods
Displayed in shop windows
Without buying everything
A box placed on an outside windowsill
For growing flowers
The glass filling this opening
Have broken this window
Sparkling leaves
In the evening sun
A waterfall, a trimming of lace
Or other material
In loose waves, like a waterfall
Outside our window
Turning the back garden
Into Heaven's paradise.

Unexpected

Petals of love
Are pouring from above
As Angels circle
And care for us
Letting us know
Their thoughts and feelings
Towards us
Making this room
Calm and peaceful
A haven of happiness.

Hand-Shake

The room is full
Crowded
With spiritual beings
A busy place
Comforting
And showing their presence
To show
You are not forgotten.

Crowd

Dancing, nattering
Guarding the house
Looking after
Friends and loved ones
You are not alone
But are being watched
And cared for.

Thunder

'I love you' she said
And his eyes lit up
Over the storm.

Surprise

The evening sun
Brights up my life
Complete meditation
Brings joy and happiness
Reflection of my glasses
I can see
On some paper
A cloud swiftly passes
All of a sudden
The sun is back
Until a mass of fog,
Consisting of minute particles of water
Often in a frozen state
Floating in the atmosphere
Everything changes
To close both eyes momentarily
To wink, to glance
Peep, to look with the eyes
Half closed
To look with amazement
To shine unsteadily or intermittently
Warmth
A calming thought
At the beauty of nature.

Cat'hood

Black cat in the night
Reassuring
Gold studded eyes
Beaming
The house is silent
In the distant
A definite sequence of
Bell-like notes
Sounded as by
An old-fashioned Grandfather's clock
An instrument for measuring time
Operated mechanically
In or to a sleeping state
Echoing time
To keep in view
To follow the motions of
With the eyes
To observe the progress or
Maintain an interest in
Follow
To look at or
Observe
Attentively
Having eyes
Spotted
As if with eyes
As much as the eye can take in.

Footways

How can we be
Afraid of the dark
When God has given us
The sun, the stars
And the moon at night
To light our way.

Song

Home
Peace, peace, peace
Over this land
Peace, peace, peace
We do what we can
Peace over this land
Peace we do what we can
Peace, oh peace
Peace, peace, peace
Over this land
Peace over this land
Peace we do what we can
I love you Lord
Oh yes I do
I love you Lord
I wish there was more.

Song Part 2

Home
I could do.
Peace, peace, peace,
Over this land
Peace, peace, peace
We do what we can
When we are alone
We wish we were home
Home comforts we
Appreciate
When we are at home
With the Lord's love
Guiding us from above
Peace, peace, peace
Guiding us home.
Peace, peace, peace
We are not on our own.

Song Part 3

Home
Angels fly
Round about us
Bringing love
Into our mist
Peace, peace, peace
We are not alone.
Peace, peace, peace
Thank you for our home
We love you Jesus
For all you have done
You help us every day
When there is work
To be done
If only we could
Repay you
Just one tiny drop.

Song Part 4

Home
You just appreciate
All we have got
Love, Love, Love
Guiding us home
Love, Love, Love
Even when we
Are alone.
Thank you Lord Jesus
High from above
Thank you Jesus
For your unending
Love.
Sometimes we think
You are not there
But we are not
Right
Because you always care
God Bless.

Man-Made Ovary

They are going to create
Monsters
Who will hate themselves
Because they don't
Look like us.

Lazar-Like

The sun
In the sky
Brings
Heat, warmth
A red fire-ball
The star which is the gravitational centre
Around which the planets revolve
And the source of light and
Heat to our planetary system
Degree of hotness
Lazar beam
Light
Shining
On my face
An apparently healthy eye having
Nevertheless impaired vision
Radiance, breadth,
Fly or ride the beam
I look at it
With the eyes
And have to
Turn away
But only
For a moment
To let it rest
On my cheek
The world
Is not a bad place
After all.

Michael

Gentle hands
Holding baby
Sheer love in his eyes
Baby feeling comfort
Safely wrapped
In his cocoon.

Crystals

The beautiful icy sea
Music, melody
From the sparkling waves
Rolling over
Then smashing on the shore
Footprints in the sand
Covered up by the tide
Seagulls floating on the water
Bouncing up and down
By the current
White foam
Creeping up the beach
The rocks are glistening with pride
As they watch the water surround them
Deep blue and green
And a soft white
Bubbles along the shore.

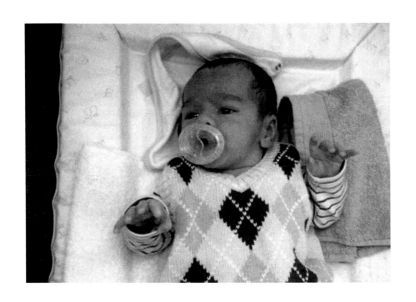

54